John Howard Wainwright

Rhymings

John Howard Wainwright

Rhymings

ISBN/EAN: 9783337124588

Printed in Europe, USA, Canada, Australia, Japan

Cover: Foto ©Thomas Meinert / pixelio.de

More available books at **www.hansebooks.com**

CONTENTS.

	PAGE
JOY BELLS,	7
CUPID AND PSYCHE,	12
LONG AGO,	14
THE LYRE OF LOVE,	16
ANIMA MEA,	18
TO DELILAH,	19
DE PROFUNDIS CLAMAVI,	23
THE SEWING GIRL'S SONG,	26
ABSENCE,	27
THE BLIND BOY TO HIS BROTHER IN CHURCH,	29
A FAREWELL,	30
THE BROOK,	33
WED NOT FOR GOLD,	35
"I BRING THEE, LOVE, NO COSTLY GEMS,"	38

	PAGE
FALSE CHARITY,	40
"NEVER DESPAIR,"	45
"I SAW HER FIRST AMID A THRONG,"	47
THE FORSAKEN,	51
OUR FATHERS,	52
THE FUTURE,	54
THE TEMPLE OF WAR, AND THE TEMPLE OF PEACE,	58
A COMETARY,	61
THE SEXTON,	64
A SERENADE,	68
NAIL OUR FLAG TO THE MAST,	70
SPRING TIME,	73
THE YACHTMAN'S SONG,	75
SAM,	77
TEDDY O'MURPHY,	79
SONGS, ETC., FROM RIP VAN WINKLE,	81

RHYMINGS.

———◆◆◆———

JOY BELLS.

ARK to the merry bells,
 As in yon tall tower they ring;
 What is the tale their muſic tells?
 What is the ſong they ſing?
Knell! Knell! Knell!
Liſt to the ſong of the bell,
"Whoever thou art;
 Of a breaking heart
And blighted hopes we tell."

"Enter in at the porch,"
 The joy-bells ſeem to ſhout,
'Tis an auction-room, and not a church,
Though no red flag hangs out.

JOY BELLS.

Sold! Sold! Sold!
The tale has been often told—
Body and heart,
Like a flave at the mart,
Bartered away for gold.

In bridal garb arrayed,
Though the rofe from her cheek has fled,
At the altar-foot ftands a lovely maid,
And wifhes fhe were dead!
Tears! tears! tears!
Heart tears, though the lids are dry:
There's hell in the foul of that maiden fair—
On her pallid lips a lie.

With eyes all glaffy and dull,
By her fide a grey-beard old,
Of figures his head like a ledger full,
His heart a lump of gold.
Oh, man, with fifter dear,
Oh, man, with mother and wife,
'Tis not a bridal you witnefs here,
But—the death of a fair young life.

He, who had won her heart,
In happy days gone by,

Now ſtandeth in the gloom apart,
All ſad and mournfully.
Cruſhed! Cruſhed! Cruſhed!
For a little golden duſt,
His joys all fled,
His hopes all dead,
A noble ſpirit loſt.

Sold is that fair young thing—
If not her heart, her hand;
Alas! what power could ſhe bring
Againſt a ſire's command?
Bartered away and ſold,
Body and heart, for gold—
Bartered away,
To that dotard grey,
For the damning greed of gold.

There ſide by ſide they ſtand,
Repeating the vows by turns;
He places a ring on that marble hand,
And the hoop, like fire, burns.
Love! Honor! Obey!
Say the lips, but the heart is dumb.
She fain would weep, ſhe tries to pray,
But nor prayers nor tears will come.

1*

Behind the altar-rail,
In accents fweet and clear,
Binding for aye that curfed fale,
Stands the reverend auctioneer.
Going! Going! Gone—
The deed is quickly done
By that plain gold ring ;
Winter and Spring   .
For life, are joined in one.

Prayed is the laft fhort prayer,
And—joyous fight to fee—
The minifter, bleffing the happy pair,
Pockets his golden fee.
Sold! Sold! Sold!
Let the bells be fadly tolled,
Better to knell
For a funeral,
Than a barter of hearts for gold.

Gone is the bridal-train,
But the bells, with their filver tone,
Still echo through the facred fane
As I ftand there alone.

Knell! Knell! Knell!
"This feems the fong of the bell:
Some bridals are made
In heaven, 'tis faid,
But this was forged in hell."

CUPID AND PSYCHE.

AY-DREAM of youth, children of Love and
    Spring,
    Buds zephyr-culled from Heaven's celeſtial
    Bowers,
Now fallen to earth, but ſtainleſs—wandering
Through this cold, heartleſs, loveleſs world of ours ;
Ah ! know ye not the bud muſt change to flower,
The flower wither ere the day grows old,
Your goſſamer woof of love hath not the power
To guard from burning noon, from evening cold.

The morning ſtars pale with the ſun's awaking ;
The morning ſkies bluſh with his coming ray ;
The morning-glories, dew-drops from them ſhaking,
Wither and droop, and cloſe at early day.

The matin song of birds from nest upspringing,
Wakes us from dreams of happy coming years;
Their vesper chaunts now tremulously singing,
Echo 'mid cypress boughs, of woe and tears.

Then cull your flowers while the dawn still lingers,
Dream love-dreams still, ye'll waken all too soon;
Hid 'neath the leaves, sharp thorns will pierce your
   fingers;
Blossoms and dreams will vanish ere the noon;
The tempest wrack shall cloud the sky ere even;
The lightning rend the giant oak in twain;
Wand'rers from Paradise, fly back to Heaven,   .
There seek, there find eternal love again.

LONG AGO.

DOST' thou remember, lady fair,
  The willow by the river fide?
One eve we fat together there
    You promifed to become my bride.
But ftay, fair lady, fpeak it not,—
  Thy anfwer I already know;
Thofe happy hours are all forgot,
  For it was very long ago.

Doft call to mind the graffy lane,
  All hidden in the little grove,—
Can memory bring it back again?
    'Twas there I told thee of my love!
Thy willing hand was clafped in mine,
  Thy lips,— fay, did they anfwer No?
'Tis paft! and why fhould I repine,—
  For it was very long ago.

Doſt call to mind the trembling kiſs
   I preſſed upon thy burning cheek?
Haſt thou forgot the words of bliſs
   Thine eyes did look, thy voice did ſpeak?
Nay, lady, do not weep! Thy tears
   Have now no right for me to flow.
I thought to ſhare thy hopes and fears,—
   But it was very long ago.

The willow by the ſtream is dead,
   The graſſy lane, the grove, both gone,—
And thou art to another wed!
   I wander through the world alone.
Yet oft unbidden burſts a ſigh,
   And down my cheeks in ſorrow flow
The tears I weep for days gone by,
   And memories of long ago.

THE LYRE OF LOVE.

"Θέλω λεγειν Ατρειδας."
ANACREON.

I STRIVE to fing of many a theme,
     As o'er the ftrings my fingers move,
But hufhed and filent is the ftream
     Of mufic, till my fong is Love.

To lay of Sorrow firft I ftruck
     The lyre that once breathed mufic fweet,
Each chord, when touched, that inftant broke,—
     It would not e'en one note repeat.

Ambition next for theme I chofe,
     But filent ftill the lyre remained;
It feemed as if in Death repofe
     Each breathlefs found and chord was chained.

I'll fing of Friendfhip, then I faid,
　　This theme at leaft will break the charm;
The lyre at Friendfhip's call was dead,—
　　E'en this the fpell could not difarm.

Joy! Thou fhalt wake my fong, I cried,—
　　In vain! no melody was there;
The ftubborn harp a moment fighed,
　　Then ceafed, as if in mute defpair.

One effort more,—of Love I'll fing,
　　Again the tunelefs lyre I'll try;
I took the harp, I touched the string,
　　Acrofs the wires my fingers fly;

And then in wild, ecftatic fire,
　　The mufic ran the chords along;
I whifpered, as I kiffed the lyre,
　　Henceforth I'll fing no other fong.

SK me not why I love thee, 'twere as well
Queſtion the roſes why they love the rain ;
Or bid the trailing morning-glories tell
Why, when the Orient Heaven puts on again
Its rainbow tabard, heralding the day,
They ope their petals, heavy with the dew.
Anima Mea, I can only ſay,
My waking ſoul roſe upward in the blue
Ether of thy dear preſence, from the earth,
Where it had lain like ſky-lark through the night
Of all my former life ; and, breaking forth
In ecſtaſies of ſuch a new delight,
It could but mount and ſing ; what though the heaven
Were far too diſtant for its flagging wing,
And it muſt, drooping, fall to earth ere even ;
What though paſt joys are ſadly vaniſhing,
And tempeſt clouds drive 'twixt me and the plain,
I ne'er can find my meadow-neſt again.

TO DELILAH.

YES! all are here, the once prized gifts,
　　Now valuelefs as withered flowers;
And Mem'ry for a moment lifts
　　The curtain from that paft of ours.
That paft, when, as before fome fhrine,
　　Where but the holieft vows are given,
My heart, to that falfe heart of thine
　　Knelt down and prayed, methought to Heaven.

Aye, prayed to Heaven! my love for thee
　　A flight of rainbow fteps did feem,
Down which God's Angels came to me
　　And whifpered, as in Jacob's dream.
The dream is paft—the flumber o'er;
　　Around me, but a defert plain;
Thou art, what thou hadft been before,
　　And I—well, I am free again.

All, faid I?　No! thou haft retained
　　The only things I craved of thee;
Oh give them back again; tho' ftained,
　　They are of pricelefs worth to me.
Yes, here the book, and here the gem
　　Lefs beauteous and lefs falfe than thou.
Ah! why didft not return with them
　　The ardent hopes, all vanifhed now.

Oh, give again thofe ardent hopes,
　　Loft beacons of my wafted years;
Bereft of them, the future opes
　　A barren wafte, all mift and tears.
Give back the truth I plighted thee;
　　Give back the trufting Love I gave;
Or fhipwrecked on life's ftormy fea,
　　I fink beneath the o'erwhelming wave.

And thou wouldft have me, too, return
　　Each record of thofe happy days?
Well doft thou know that I would fcorn
　　To treafure ftill thefe mockeries?
I fend thee each material trace
　　Of what thou wert, of what thou art;
Would 'twere as eafy to efface
　　And blot thine image from my heart.

Here is the tress of golden hair
   I took from off thy snowy brow;
Is not the kiss still lingering there?
   Dost thou not feel it burning now?
Thou may'st erase that kiss no more
   Than human hand can wash the blood
Of murder'd Rizzio from the floor
   Of Mary's bower in Holy Rood.

Oh! I am powerless to deal
   With life, for thou hast made me weak.
Thy kiss, Delilah, still I feel,
   Thy lying kiss upon my cheek.
Yet still from slumber I awake,
   And hurl this thraldom from my mind;
Thus, traitress, thus thy bonds I break,
   And thank my God I am not blind.

What's this? a tear! well, let it fall,
   'Tis not the first, 'twill be the last:
And with it, now I banish all
   My thought of thee, thine hour is past!
'Twas near two thousand years ago—
   The tale is old; hast thou not read
How Judas bought perdition so,
   And with a kiss his Lord betrayed?

Room for the Leper! tho' the crowd
  May yield due homage to thy ſtate,
And cringe and ſmile, in anguiſh bowed
  Thy foul ſhall ſit without the gate.
Perchance thou may'st conceal thy ſhame,
  Poor leman, from the world unſeen,
Thy heart ſhall utter ſtill the ſame
  Foul leper's cry, " Unclean! unclean!"

Thou hadſt thy price, and it is paid;
  That peerleſs form of thine is ſold.
Hearts were not mentioned in the trade,
  They ſell for love,—but thou for gold.
Bought is thy life—thy hand—thy face,—
  A perjured vow—a ring—and then
Bought is each loving, fond embrace;
  Thou'rt but a wedded Magdalen.

I almoſt pity thee thy fate,
  Life fettered, like a galley-ſlave;
In anguiſh thou ſhalt ſeek, too late,
  Some power to ſuccor and to ſave.
Too late on earth; the anointed feet
  Need not thy tears, thy golden hair;
He ſits upon the mercy feat—
  Perchance thou'lt find forgiveneſs there.

DE PROFUNDIS CLAMAVI.

COME, home at laft,
　　Weary and cold,
　　Poor, weak, and old,
　　Bending beneath the weight of forrows paft,
Blind to the gifts of mercy manifold,
Looking out on the vaft
Unfathomable ocean of To Come.
Hopes now all vanifhed, earthly joys all paft,
Groping with outftretched arms amid the gloom,
And clouds of doubt hung round for auguries
Of that dear promife, which upon the Crofs
Our Saviour gave the finner at his fide.
Our Saviour, mine! yes, 'twas for me He died.
In that dread hour he hears the finner's cries;
In that dread hour he liftens, and replies,
"Thou art forgiven,
　　Count other gain but lofs.

With faltering footsteps follow me to Heaven ;
Turn from the earth, look upward to the skies,
To-day thou'lt be with me in Paradise."

Home, home at last,
Weighed down with pain ;
The dust and travel stain
Of wasted years hang heavy on my brow ;
Earth's choicest gifts but dust and ashes now.
Bending beneath a burthen I would fain
Lay at His feet whose vast
And boundless mercy held me up so long ;
Yet at those bleeding feet I dare not cast
My heavy load.   Were they not pierced for me ?
Did he not hang upon the 'cursed tree ?
Redeeming me ; while I—I held the spear
That pierced His side ;
I crowned the reed with gall ;
I mocked and scourged, reviled and crucified ;
And dare I now at this last hour call
On Him for aid, now at the set of sun,
My work time over, and the daylight gone ?
When in my hand, sole offering, I bring
A buried talent to my God and King ?
Dying on Cross, the Saviour still replies,
"To-day thou'lt be with me in Paradise."

Home, home at laſt,
Humbly repenting,
Father, relenting,
Take to thy arms again an erring ſon,
At my great ſinfulneſs ſtand not aghaſt.
Jeſus, my Saviour, be thou, too, conſenting :
Thou who didſt tell the Prodigal's return.
I have ſadly paſſed
The years ſince firſt I left thee, wandering far
From Home and Thee, without the guiding ſtar
Of thy dear teachings ;—heavineſs and pain
Have travelled with me ; now I come again,
Praying thy pardon for the gifts I've waſted,
Aſking forgiveneſs for the ill-ſpent years.
Brimming with ſweetneſs ſeemed the cup I taſted,
But oh! the dregs were bitterneſs and tears.
Canſt thou forgive me ?
See me humbly kneeling ;
Jeſus, my Saviour, oh again receive me,
Liſten to my agonized appealing ;
I read thy promiſe on the weſtern ſkies,
"To-day thou'lt be with me in Paradiſe."

2

THE SEWING GIRL'S SONG.

EARILY, wearily ſtitching,
From morning till late in the night,
To make ſome young lady bewitching,
Whoſe heart, beating light
'Neath the robe that we ſew,
Never, never will know,
Why the tiſſue ſo bright
Is dimmed here and there,
And perchance would not care
Were ſhe told that our tears
Make each ſpot that appears
Like a ſtain on the ſtuff.
But enough, girls, enough;
Your needles keep plying,
We are not paid for crying.

ABSENCE.

USHED is my harp, as o'er its unftrung chords
My fingers idly fweep, the burning words
That echo in my heart, vainly effay
To murmur on my lip. Through the long day
My flagging mind is powerlefs but to turn
And dream of vaniflied joys. I can but mourn
Thy abfence, as we mourn the flowers departed,
And fummer paft. I thought to be ftrong-hearted,
When thou wert gone, and hurry back again
To the cold world. But vain the ftruggle, vain
Are all my efforts. Round me is a fpell
Like that with which the moon, as poets tell,
Guides every motion of the ftormy fea;
So in my thought I can but follow thee;—
And as, when all around is raylefs night,
In one long golden line of love and light
The moon is mirrored in its heaving breaft,
So in my heart thy image is impreffed.

Pale Dian calmly fits enthroned on high,
Peerlefs amid the ftars, while toward the fky
The fea lifts up its waves as if in prayer,
Afking a fmile, and fhe all coldly there
Looks down unconfcious.   Lady, did the gleam
Of thy dark eyes upon thy lover beam
As coldly bright ?   Or did their lids conceal
How much, though calm the brow, the heart could
       feel ?
As the poor cripple, through long weary years
Of pain and anguifh lay, 'mid hopes and fears,
Waiting the Angel-vifitant to cool
And ftir the waters of Bethefda's pool,
Whofe troubled wave fhould give him health once
       more—
Thus my lone heart fits idly by the fhore
Of the dim future, waiting thy return ;
And when on weftern hills at funfet, burn
Beacons of bright To-morrows, toward the fky
My eyes I turn; and when I fee on high
'Mid twilight's gloom the crefcent moon appear,
I dream the pool is ftirred, the angel draweth near.

THE BLIND BOY TO HIS BROTHER
IN CHURCH.

I AM not blind, dear Brother, now,
    For, though I cannot fee—
Though darknefs overfpreads my brow—
    The Gofpel fhines for me.

Lift, Brother, lift! each holy word
    Is graven on my mind;
I could not fee, but then I heard,—
    Brother, I am not blind!

Father! to whom all fuppliants kneel,
    I afk not worldly fight;
Oh, hear a poor blind boy's appeal
    For more of Heavenly light!

A FAREWELL.

FAREWELL ! Farewell! I fcarce can bring
    My trembling lips to fpeak the word;
Its hated accents feem to ring
    Like funeral chimes by mourners heard;
It drags me from the dreamy paft,—
    Of buried hopes it tolls the knell,
And happinefs retreats aghaft
    Before the dreaded word—Farewell!

No more of love, no more of home,
    No more of every joy I prize,
The parting hour at length has come,
    And even friendfhip withering dies.
No more ! What thoughts of deep defpair
    Thofe bitter words of anguifh tell!
No hope of future refting there,
    To light the fadnefs of Farewell!

Adieu! To thee I will not speak
 Of what I fancied once might be,—
'Twould bring a blush upon thy cheek,
 In pity for my misery.
I will not claim the single tear
 Thou couldst not hide, were I to tell
Of what thou need'st not, must not, hear,—
 'Tis whispered in this last Farewell!

Perchance, when ocean rolls between,
 Thou'lt sometimes kindly think of one,
Forgetting what he would have been,—
 Remember only he is gone.
Perchance, when all around seems gay,
 Thy thoughts may for a moment dwell
On him who must not, dare not stay,
 But bids thee now a last Farewell!

Adieu! adieu! I meant to go
 With changeless cheek and tearless eye,
Nor deemed 'twould wring my spirit so,
 To speak one little word—Good-bye!
I thought to wear a careless smile,
 And with a merry laugh to tell—
Although my heart should break, the while—
 Some idle jest, and then—Farewell!

Yet, fare thee well!   I ne'er ſhall bend
   My knee at morn and eve in prayer,
But ſupplications ſhall afcend
   For thee to Heaven, entreating there
That angel hands may round thee twine
   A wreath of happineſs, a ſpell
Of ſunny hours, that conſtant ſhine,
   Nor ever bid, as I, Farewell!

THE BROOK.

FLASHING, daſhing, comes the rill,
    Rumbling, tumbling, down the hill,
    Swollen with the winter ſnows,
    Swifter on its courſe it goes,
Flinging gems on buſh and ſprav,
As it paſſes on its way
To the ice-encumbered river,
Where its drops are loſt forever
In the ſwollen tide that runs
To the South, where tropic ſuns,
While it knows not of its danger,
Warm to melt the northern ſtranger.
Stopping, as it comes along,
To repeat its little ſong,
In the pool it loves to linger,
While Jack Froſt, with fairy finger,
   2*

Strives to bind it in his net,
Fain would lead it to forget
That it ftill muft on, though weary,
On, through the world, though cold and dreary,
On, though it leaves all joy behind it;
On, though the Sirens ftrive to bind it;
To the great Gulf it ftill muft flee,—
The river of Eternity.

WED NOT FOR GOLD.

OULDST wed for gold ?   Seek yonder palace-
gate,
Where liveried menials at the entrance wait ;
They guard the porch 'gainft all of low degree,
But thou, unfeen, fhalt enter there with me,
And learn a leffon from a gilded page ;
Too true the tale it tells, from age to age,
Of wealth and mifery joining hand in hand.
See yonder lady fair ; would'ft underftand
Why on her youthful brow that fhadow refts ?
Can it be true that aught of grief molefts
One who is miftrefs of a home like this ?
What ! can not riches buy e'en earthly blifs ?
Fool ! lift the moral that this fcene imparts :
She purchafed wealth—with what—two broken hearts !
Scarce one fhort year ago, a youthful pair
Plighted their troth, and fwore through life to fhare,
Whether for weal or woe, a mutual lot ;

But wealth came riding by, and she forgot
Her faith, his love ; alas ! poor girl, she sold
His earthly happiness, her Heaven, for gold !
Where is he now, that poor heart-broken boy ?
When he beheld his all of earthly joy
Gone, gone for ever with the rich man's bride,—
The church-yard tells the mournful tale—" he died."
And is she happy now ?   No ; every scene
She looks upon but tells what might have been.
Though decked in costly silks and satins rare,
Though priceless jewels glitter in her hair,
Though blessed with every thing that wealth can buy,
Still, is she happy ?   Lift the stifled sigh
Bursting unbidden from her aching breast !
It sometimes finds a voice, though oft repressed ;
And in that sigh a truthful tale is told :
Go, write it on thy heart, then wed for gold !

Wouldst wed for gold ?   Seek yonder humble cot ;
There wealth and misery are alike forgot ;
Wide open stands the hospitable door,
And welcome he who enters, rich or poor ;
Contentment smiles around with homely grace ;
Here jaundiced Avarice with saffron face
Would e'en forget his hoards of yellow dust,
And give his millions, could he share the crust

That honeſt labor renders ever ſweet,
(Not always ſuch the luxuries of the great).
See from his daily toil the cotter come :
Full well he knows the loved one waits him home ;
Little cares he to ſhare the rich man's part,
His mine of wealth is one true woman's heart ;
Like thoſe twin ſtars that mariners deſcry
When looking Heavenward in the northern ſky,
They ſeek the Polar Star to track their way
O'er pathleſs ſeas, but, leſt they wandering ſtray
And chooſe ſome other orb, the Pointers guide
To it alone, heedleſs of all beſide ;
Revolving ever, ſtill they never rove
From out the path that guards the ſtar they love.
So woman's rich affections, pure and true,
Once gained, will ever fondly cling to you,
Though all elſe change.   Let good or ill betide,
Faint not, bleſt man, an angel's at thy ſide !
Conſtant in death, ſhe whiſpering points above :
" Deareſt, we'll meet in Heaven, for Heaven is love."
Think well on this, ye fools that ſeek to gain
A fleeting pleaſure for an age of pain !
'Tis ſhort-lived pleaſure wealth alone can give,
And happier far, methinks, 'twould be to live
Poor but contented.   Now my tale is told ;
Go, write it on thy heart, then wed for gold !

"I BRING THEE, LOVE, NO COSTLY GEMS."

BRING thee, love, no coſtly gems,
   To decorate thy golden hair,
Freſh flowers are Nature's diadems,—
   Then let them bloom in fragrance there.

The wave-waſhed Pearl, from ocean caves,
   The Indian Ruby's roſeate dye,
The Diamond, frozen tear of ſlaves,
   Were dim beſide thy ſparkling eye!

The Opal, rainbow-kiſſed, may lend
   Freſh charms to many a form leſs bright,
But jewels, love, would vainly blend
   With thine that aſk no borrowed light!

Then take the Rofe, its funfet hue
   A fleeting blufh upon thy cheek,—
The Heliotrope, whofe modeft blue
   Seems ever of thine eyes to fpeak.

The Lily on thine ivory brow,
   Contrafted with its fnowy white,
Were dull,—then, love, I pray thee now,
   Enwreathe thy hair with flowers to-night.

FALSE CHARITY.

AYE! give your thoufands in an idle caufe,
　　Break through your fathers' and your country's
　　　　laws,
　　Forget the precepts once fo dearly prized,
Be all your former principles defpifed!
But, while ye drain your hoards for other lands,
Can ye be blind to what your own demands?
Can ye o'erlook the many fuffering poor
Who beg their daily bread from door to door?
Pleading the tafk of aiding foreign flaves,
Deny to them the mite their hunger craves!
Beftowing millions on fome project wild,
Refufe a penny to a famifhed child!
All this ye do, vain fools!—all this, and more!
And is it Charity that claims your ftore?
Afk yourfelves this; draw back the mifty vail
That hides your hearts,—let confcience tell the tale.

Does aught of charity the gold fupply?
What, no refponfe! Wilt give me no reply?
Then I will anfwer truly for ye all:
'Tis Pride!—the fin that caufed an angel's fall!
'Tis Pride!—that hurled a holy fpirit down
From higheft Heaven, and caufed a God to frown
On thofe he loved the deareft, beft, before!
Oh, fearch your hearts, and gather from your ftore
At leaft the crumbs, and give them to the poor.
'Twas but an hour ago I faw a form
That dragged fcarce half a body through the ftorm,
'Twixt bending crutches, flowly on his way,
From clofing door and clofing door, to pray
A little aid, to fave his only fon;
And unaffifted, ftill he tottered on.
I know not if 'twas pity bade me fpeak,—
I could not help it, for he looked fo weak,
Methought that every ftep would be his laft;
He feemed to ftagger in the wintry blaft
As if he had not ftrength to hold him up.
Poor man! he muft have drained the bitter cup
Of pain and penury e'en to the dregs!—
And now—the hardeft pang of all—he begs
From men of wealth a mite, to fave his boy,—
Not for himfelf,—no! fooner far deftroy
His hated life, and end at once his woe;

But for his child he will defcend fo low,
And cringe to avarice, can he only fave
His chiefeft joy and blefling from the grave.
Lift to the tale he tells!—Columbians, hear!
And for the love of all you hold moft dear,
Forget it not.—Remember thofe at home.
Firft give to thefe, then let your pity roam
O'er all the world;—chief in your hearts fhould be
Your country's claims,—not thofe beyond the fea!
" Six years ago went up a mighty cry,
From North and South, of War and Liberty.
With many thoufands more I took the field,
Refolved to die or conquer, ne'er to yield ;
In many a battle willingly I fhed
My blood like rain.   A brother left I dead,
On Cerro Gordo's fanguinary plain ;
At Cherubufco's fight I ftood again,
Clofe by another ; he, too, dying, fell
E'en at my feet!   O God!   I loved him well!—
Yet on, ftill on, I preffed, till—harder lot—
I, too, fell—wounded by a cruel fhot ;—
Which left me as you fee, yet killed me not.—
A helplefs, ufelefs, broken-hearted man,
At laft I gained my home."   Hear this who can,
And check the blood that mantles o'er your brow :
His grateful country has forgot him now,—

His withered laurel has to cyprefs turned ;—
From ev'ry door the wounded man is fpurned,
While eager hands throw down the heaps of gold
Before a felf-made idol,—as of old,
When Ifrael at Jehovah dared to laugh,
And gave their wealth to build a molten calf.
But lift the tale : "I gained my native land,
Maimed, and in want. Of all that ftalwart band
Who, but a year before, went forth in pride,
But few remained,—the greater part had died .
Of fell difeafe ; or, on the battle-field,
Face to the foe. Columbia's fame was fealed
And figned in blood ! Wives, parents, children, mourn
Loved ones departed, never to return !
Full many a widow welcomed us with tears ;
Our grateful country welcomed us with cheers,—
Then gave us—to requite the blood we fhed—
Medals !—which we were forced to fell for bread !
Aye ! fell for bread ; no other means remained,
To ftay our hunger.—Medals, bravely gained,
For food and raiment ! " God, in whom I truft,
Are fuch things true ? Can it be right or juft
To aid each ufelefs and chimeric fcheme
With wafted thoufands ? Strive to fill a ftream
With drops of water till it flood its banks,
Repay a friend's devotednefs with thanks ;

Attempt to curb the whirlwind with thine arm ;
Preach love to tigers, filence to the ftorm,—
When thefe ye do, 'tis time enough to free
The fhackled nations by thy charity.
Begin at home—there's many an object here
Has claims upon thy bounty, far more near
Than thofe ye aid fo freely, far more dear
To every honeft, patriotic heart,—
Claims that are preffed with no rhetoric art,
But plead in withered frames, and funken eyes !
Delay no longer, left another dies
Ere ye refolve.   Hafte, hafte, the hours fly faft !
Though late, determine to be juft, at laft.

"NEVER DESPAIR."

EVER defpair! Prefs ahead on thy way,
 Fear not though the clouds lower darkling to-
  day,
 Fear not though thy heart is encurtained in
  gloom,
Prefs onward! To-morrow the funfhine may come.
The day-ftar is there, and ere long 'twill be fhining,
The Heavens are blue, then away with repining.
The pathway before thee, though fteep, is ftill open,
Prefs on! though the road may be rugged and broken:
You ne'er can replenifh a light purfe with grieving,
Then let a light heart be the balance relieving;
'Twill weigh down the purfe and e'en make you forget it,
'Twill fill it, perchance, if you only will let it.
A heart that is light is a true golden treafure,
For it joys in itfelf, nor looks elfewhere for pleafure.
'Tis a fun ever fhining on all who are near it;
'Tis a fweet playing lute to whoever may hear it;

'Tis a mirror reflecting all others in gladnefs;
'Tis a curtain to hang o'er the dark brow of fadnefs;
A diamond that fhines, though furrounded in gloom;
A lamp to illumine the mifts of the tomb.
Never defpair!   Life yet is remaining,
To give thee frefh chance of the vict'ry obtaining.
Far, far in the diftance hope beckons thee on,
Think not of the idle days faded and gone.
Think not of thy former misfortunes with forrow,
Refolve to retrieve them to-day and to-morrow.
Though friends may forfake thee, the cold world be
          frowning,
Prefs on! and fuccefs fhall thy efforts be crowning.
Prefs on! for the fun in thy fky foon may fet,
Then wafte not the moments in ufelefs regret;
No time now is left to reflect on loft chances,
Thy life every hour to its ending advances.
Let all thy tranfactions be honeft and fair,
And e'en let thy watchword be, " Never Defpair!"

"I SAW HER FIRST AMID A THRONG."

I SAW her firſt amid a throng
   Of gallants brave and ladies fair ;
Hers was the gayeſt, happieſt ſong—
   She was the brighteſt being there.

A happy ſmile played 'round her mouth,
   Like ſunſhine on a placid lake
When zephyrs from the ſunny South
   The golden-dimpled ripples wake.

I ſcarcely dared to aſk the name
   Of her who ſeemed ſo fair and bright,
Yet to my brow the heart-blood came,
   As near me oft ſhe paſſed that night.

We met again, and I had known
 On life's dark ocean many a ſtorm;
Full many a year had ſwiftly flown,—
 And oh! how changed that angel form!

The hand of Death was on her brow,
 So low her voice ſhe ſcarce could ſpeak;
Her hazel eye was ſunken now,
 And pallid the once roſy cheek,—

Save where a deep carnation fluſh
 Was ſhining on the ſnowy white;
I knew it was a flower whoſe bluſh
 Foretold the quickly coming night.

'Twas on the rolling deep we met,
 She ſought for health a ſunnier ſhore,
But ere the ſecond ſun had ſet,
 Her pilgrimage of life was o'er.

Yet ſtill that happy ſmile was there;
 Cold, heartleſs Death forgot his power,
And pitying, reſolved to ſpare
 The beauty of the withered flower.

Poor girl! alas, no tree fhall wave
   Its drooping branches o'er thy head,
For fathomlefs the ocean grave
   Where thou waft calmly, fadly laid.

No love-fown flower e'er fhall bloom
   Above the fpot where thou doft fleep ;
No fculptured ftone fhall mark thy tomb,
   For friends to wander there and weep.

Yet many a heart enfhrines thee ftill,
   And many a thought and tear are given,
While hopes, rich hopes, each bofom fill,
   To meet thy angel foul in Heaven.

I faw her once again in dreams,
   And very oft thofe dreams return ;
An angel all of light fhe feems,
   And, fmiling, bids me ceafe to mourn.

She points her finger toward the fkies,
   And bids me look in faith above,
Seek there a Bride that never dies,
   A heaven of unending love.

3

Yes, angel, yes ! though diftant far
   From friends, and home, and all I ftray,
Thou art the radiant Beacon ftar
   That guides my wavering, wandering way.

THE FORSAKEN.

I FEEL no more thy cruel art,
　　And bid adieu with tearlefs eye;
I cannot free again my heart,
　　But I can let it break and die.
Perchance I e'en fhall ftrive to fmile,
　　When thou art to another wed;
But I implore thee, wait awhile,
　　Nor claim thy bride till I am dead.

I thought not thus the dream would end,—
　　Oh, 'twas a hard and bitter waking!
But ceafe thy falfenefs to defend,
　　Go and forget the heart now breaking.
The evening fun may rife to-morrow,
　　The parting fhip return to fhore,
Alas my hopes have fet in forrow,
　　Have fet to rife again no more.

OUR FATHERS.

LONG time they bore oppreſſion uncomplained,
    Long time, till tyranny deſpotic reigned,
    Till they could bear no longer, and they prayed
    Unto the God of battles for His aid.
And then they all in ſolemn concert ſwore,
Never to reſt until from out their ſhore,
They'd cleanſed the ſtain that o'er it like a pall
Of death and blackneſs hung, and till through all
The length and breadth of their loved land the rays
Of Liberty's bright ſunſhine drove the haze
And dark cloud of oppreſſion o'er the main,
Back to proud Albion's ſhores in haſte again.
And as the prairie when the firebrand
Has touched its border, ſo o'er all the land,
When once the torch of liberty was fired,
The flames quick ran along unquenched, untired.

Then men, their country's ornament and pride,
For freedom fought and bled, for freedom died.
'To cleanfe Columbia of that tyrant band,
The ploughman left the ploughfhare, feized the brand,
The ftatefman for the gun, the pen refigned ;
And young and old, and rich and poor combined,
Left home and firefide for the battle-field,
Refolved to die or conquer, ne'er to yield ;
Refolved to drive the oppreffor from the land :
And though but few, that brave, undaunted band
O'ercame the tyrant in his ftrength and might,
And conquered, for their caufe was juft and right,
That prayer for aid was anfwered, they fuftained,
By God's affiftance, Independence gained,
And left to us, whofe proudeft boaft fhould be—
Our fathers died to fet their country free.

THE FUTURE.

HE dim and fhadowy Future!—who can fay
What is the Future? Not one fingle day
Canft thou, O mortal, fcan the great " To
 Come ! "
We know the grave muft be our final home
Upon this earth, and that is all we know ;
Along the paft we look—as o'er the fnow
The weary traveller, turning, views each mark
His foot has made diftinct ;—but through the dark
Unknown Futurity, thou canft not peer.
Believe ! Make Hope thy guide, and let her cheer
Thy onward way ; look upward to thy GOD,
Nor ftrive to look beyond !—And when the fod
Covers the clay that now confines thy foul,
His hand fhall guide thee to the wifhed-for goal !
Trufting in Him alone ; learn from the Paft
To fhun the fnares that fin would 'round thee caft ;

Make of thy former life a well-read book,—
Inscribe it on thy heart, that thou mayst look
Upon its page whene'er thy footsteps stray;
Make it a finger-post to point the way
That thou must follow!—Read the Past aright,—
'Twill be a beacon in the darkest night,
To light the narrow path that thou shouldst tread;
The Past is for the living, not the dead!

See yonder monument that towers on high!
'Tis not alone to tell the passer by
Some patriot, sage, or hero, lies beneath,
For whom 'twas raised.   And for the laurel wreath
What cares the dead?   He cannot see it now;
He cannot wear upon his worm-seared brow
The marble chaplet that is chiselled here
Upon the stone; or feel the grateful tear
We drop upon the flower that blossoms o'er
His lifeless form.   His boat is launched from shore
Upon that fathomless and unknown sea—
The boundless ocean of Eternity!
Come; read with me the epitaph,—'twill speak
Volumes of richest teachings.   Let us seek
To know the reason why such costly pile
Tells of the dead.   What! Cynic, dost thou smile—
As if the grave-yard could no lesson tell
To such as thee?—Go thou, and read it well;

'Grave every epitaph upon thy heart,
'Twill make thee happier, wifer, than thou art.
Read this : " He was a good and honeft man ; "
Read, aye, and emulate him, if you can,—
" He loved his country, and for her he died."
Is there no leffon here ?　See, far and wide,
Your country torn by faction, and for what ?
Oh ! have ye all fo fpeedily forgot
The fea of holy blood your Fathers fhed ?
Tear down your monuments, difentomb your dead,
Scatter their afhes to the winds of Heaven !
Revile their names, and ye may be forgiven,—
But, the great Fabric they erected, fpare !
Forbear !—deluded Fools !　In time, forbear !
Once fevered, ye can never more unite
The glorious chain your Fathers forged fo bright !
Break but one link and every hope is gone,—
Not e'en the ftrongeft State can ftand alone !
What ! fhall our flag—the banner of the free—
Be furled forever o'er the boundlefs fea !
And wave no more in glory o'er the land ?
Say, would ye on your Fathers' memory brand
The damning tale that they fo bravely fought,
Through long, long years, and bled and died for naught ?
Wouldft rend afunder every well-known ftripe !—
Blot out each ftar ?　Vile Traitors ! would ye wipe

From off the book of Nations what has been,—
The nobleſt page that book has ever ſeen,—
And give one only ſtripe to every State—
One only ſtar ?   Pauſe, ere it be too late !
Think what ye do !   Look backward o'er the Paſt,—
Read there thy country's welfare,—bind her faſt
In loving bonds of Union ! let the ſun
Of Liberty its courſe of glory run.
Columbia !—My loved country, riſe again
From thy debaſement !   Waſh away the ſtain
That ſullies the bright radiance of thy face !
Curſed be thy ſons that would their land diſgrace !
Still may thy glorious ſtandard float unfurled,
Ever the pride and glory of the world !

3*

THE TEMPLE OF WAR, AND THE TEMPLE OF PEACE.

ARK! to the fhout that wakes the Eaftern world!
The flag of battle is again unfurled.
From Albion's fnow-white cliffs, from Gallia's
plain,
See fteel-clad warriors preffing o'er the main;
From gallant navies floating, fee advance
St. GEORGE's ftandard and the flag of France,
Foemen for ages, now as friends they fight,
Their mutual war-cry, "GOD defend the right!"
Hark! how with ftartling clang and horrid jar,
All rufted o'er by peace, the iron bar
That clofed the gates of JANUS falls to earth.
From its wide portals opened haften forth
The turbaned Moflem, and a hoft of fpears
From Danube's bank, and giant cuiraffiers,

Mounted on coal-black fteeds of Norman blood,
Champing the bit impatient.   Now the road
Shakes 'neath the wheels of a long rumbling train
From Strafbourg's arfenal.   A martial ftrain
Comes floating on the breeze ; then haften on
A hoft of bearded Coffacks of the Don ;
"GOD and our Church !" their watchword.   Next
    appear
The unarmed millions, betwixt hope and fear,
Straining their fetters, burning to be free,
And eager to revenge long years of tyranny.
But all in vain the eye effays to fcan
The countlefs throng, though foremoft in the van,
And mingling here and there along the line,
The Crefcent and the Crofs their folds entwine
In loving union.   Wondrous fight to fee,
Chriftian and Turk arrayed in harmony
Againft a Chriftian foe, whofe hated thrall
Is fraught with equal danger to them all !

The vifion changes, and with glad furprife,
Another picture greets our wond'ring eyes ;
Another temple's gates are oped to-day,
And to its portals flock a long array
Of peaceful warriors, ftruggling to be firft
In every art and fcience.   They have nurfed

Full many an infant thought, till it has grown
A thing of good to all; men who have known
What 'twas to fight and win—a noble band,
From diftant climes and our dear native land.
Through the long galleries and aifles we fcan
The inventive power and mafter-mind of man;
Lift to the bufy fpindles' ceafelefs hum,
Singing a fong of peace! The gorgeous loom
Sufpends on every fide with lavifh hand
The trophies of a battle far more grand
Than victory ever fmiled on.   Here we find
The bloodlefs conquefts of the immortal mind;
The embodied toil of thoufands here we view,
Showing what heads can plan and hands can do.
Each art has lent its proudeft works to grace
And fcatters gems of beauty o'er the place:
The fields, the woods, the flocks, the fea, the mine,
Their varied gifts beftow, and all combine
To pleafe and to inftruct.   Raife high the ftrain,
And let the dome reëcho back again
Our fong of triumph for the ftruggle paft,
For trials o'er, fuccefs achieved at laft!

YSTERIOUS ftranger, ftartling each ftar-
gazer!
Oh, moft *ex-orb-itant* celeftial blazer!
Tell me, I pray, of your fidereal ftatus:
Belong you to the *poſſe comet-atus*
Of heavenly fpheres, enrolled to keep the peace—
("*Argo*," a member of the Golden Fleece?)
But ftars no longer ferve in the police,
So this can't be. I think I've found you out:
You've been *tale-bearing* 'mid the ftars, no doubt,
Or, much the fame, perchance in Leflie's pay,
You've been illumining the Milky Way.
Have you made Jupiter of Juno jealous?
Earth wants enlightening, fo in Latin *tellus,*
Quaé fit cometa nemo ſibi forté,
Contentus eſt? Evenit faepe forté.

A *parallax* of rupees for an anfwer,
By *Gemini*, explain it if you *Cancer!*
Have you been ferenading female ftars?
To the intenfe difguft of pa's and *Mars*,
Who think your fparking round a bafe intrufion,
Your kiffes but *elliptical* delufion?
It may be you've eclipfed that thievifh hero,
And fome cold night fent *Mercury* towards Zero.
Or, did you wink at Venus and enrage her—
At leaft you're pointed at by Urfa Major.
Don't hope to *parfe* me with your *declination*,
I'm bent in-*tenfe*-ly on an explanation,
You cannot hide, as through the heavens you fail;
That you're a ftar, and *thereby hangs a tale.*
I've *Saturn* hour waiting for your ftory,
Though *non-Comet-al*, be *ex-planet-ory.*
I fear you've rifen above your proper ftation,
By *mean attraction* gained your *elevation*,
For fome *fpecific* caufe affumed your *gravity:*
I fee both through yourfelf and your depravity.
Why thus perfift in fuch *eccentric* courfes?
Are they internal or external forces
That guide your actions as through fpace you roll?
Do you revolve on a magnetic pole
Like this fame world of ours? I hope I *axis*
A proper queftion, for belief it taxes

To think you wander in this courfe erratic
Without *plane* reafon.   Are you *fyftematic*
In what you do?   There now, you're out of fight
Without fo much as bidding me good night.
That's very rude, but yet I gather from it,
You mean to tell me that I cannot *comet*.

THE SEXTON.

E who reflects on
   The trade of a sexton,
     Doubtless will agree
'Tis of any calling
The moſt appalling,
     That poſſibly can be.

Air crematical,
Emblematical
   Of his mournful trade,
Voice funereal,
Half miniſterial,
   Half a ring of the ſpade.

At font baptifmal,
Not as yet difmal,
 He takes his wonted place,
Sedately liftening
To every chriftening
 With kind, paternal face.

Next at the wedding,
Moft proudly treading,
 Seeming their joy to fhare,
With beaming fmile,
Along the aifle,
 He ufhers the happy pair.

To each phyfician
He bows with fubmiffion,
 And hands a black-edged card;
" If it comes in your way, fir,
A word pleafe fay, fir,
 For me: the times are hard.

" We're both of a trade—
Scalpel and fpade
 Follow each other faft;
When you get through, fir,
My work I'll do, fir,
 And truft me it will laft.

"Shrouds, coffins, hearfes,
To fuit all purfes,
 With gloves that never fit.
If you don't like black
I'll take them back
 In trade; don't mention it."

He looks around him
As if, confound him,
 He dares not fay aloud:
" 'Twill give me pleafure
To take your meafure
 And order for a fhroud."

Black gloves his hands on
When he ftands on
 Ceremonial gloom;
Head uncovered,
As if he hovered
 Still at the door of the tomb.

His eyes half clofing,
Not as if dozing,
 Standing by to drop,
With meafured dafhes,
The duft and afhes,
 Upon the coffin top.

He has his place
In life's long race
    From firſt to lateſt breath,
You'll find at laſt,
Run ſlow or faſt,
    He's ſure to be in at the death.

"Who'll be the next on
My books?" cries the ſexton ;
    "Ready by day or night;
Give me a call, ſir—
Sign of the Pall, ſir ;
    Ring the ſmall bell at the right."

A SERENADE.

THE filver orb of night
    Is fhining mild above,
  A fitting torch to light
    The holy hour of love.
       Then, deareft, wake!
       For o'er the lake
Thy lover flies to meet thee,—
       While to his oar
       The anfwering fhore
Sends echo back to greet thee.

Lift! how amid the trees
  In heavenly murmur fighs
The love-fong of the breeze,
  And every leaf replies.

Then, love, let sleep,
No longer keep
Those bright eyes from thy lover,—
But lend their light
To glad the night,
Ere night's sweet reign is over.

List! how upon the strand
  The rippling wavelets break;
They whisper to the land
  The love-tale of the lake.
    An hour like this
    Is made for bliss,
Oh, leave me not forsaken,—
    Below, above,
    All, all is love,
Then 'waken, love, awaken!

NAIL OUR FLAG TO THE MAST.

AIL our flag to the maſt! while the bunting is
new,
   And our ſhip in the roadſtead lies ready for
ſailing,
Her rigging is ſtrong, and her compaſs is true,
   And we fear not the foe or the tempeſts prevailing,
      Her keel was well laid,
      Her maſts are well ſtayed,
   And of live Yankee oak every timber is made ;
Then wooed by the zephyr or rent by the blaſt,
We'll ſteer on our courſe with flag nailed to the maſt.

Nail our flag to the maſt, ere the breaking of day,
   To catch the firſt beam of the ſun at its riſing ;
Then our ſails ſheeted home, and the anchor aweigh,
   We'll ſtart from the land, every danger deſpiſing.

Though the fierce tempeft wrack
Follow faft on our track,
Right onward we'll prefs, nor at danger look back;
And over the billow our bark fhall fly faft,
With the ftars and the ftripes firmly nailed to the maft.

Nail our flag to the maft! then blow high or blow low,
Come funfhine or ftorm, ftill that banner fo peerlefs
Shall wave o'er our heads as right onward we go,
For our feamen are ftanch and our captain is fearlefs.
Though in fhreds every fail
Shall be rent by the gale,
Not a heart fhall defpond, not a cheek fhall turn pale;
But we'll work with a will till the danger is paft,
We're fafe, come what may, with flag nailed to the maft.

Nail our flag to the maft! that all nations may know
It floats over freemen who'll ever defend it,
Will ne'er haul it down, though o'erwhelming the foe,
Though the fmoke may enfhroud, though the war hail
may rend it.
When the fmoke clears away
At the clofe of the fray,
Our flag, though in tatters, we'll proudly difplay
And e'en though we fink, ftill unconquered at laft,
We'll fink 'neath the wave with flag nailed to the maft.

Nail our flag to the maſt! 'Tis the flag of the free,
  While the deeds of our fathers are hallowed in ſtory,
Our ſtandard a terror to tyrants ſhall be,
    To freemen a beacon of honor and glory.
        Spite of wind and of rain,
        On its folds not a ſtain,
      Our flag ſhall untarniſhed forever remain ;
In peace or in war, from the firſt to the laſt,
Dear country, ſpeed on, with flag nailed to the maſt.

Nail our flag to the maſt ! In the morning of youth,
  Ere the ſky of our life is o'erclouded by ſorrow,
Make Honor our watchword, our beacon-ſtar Truth ;
    Let defeat for to-day teach ſucceſs for to-morrow.
        Thus true to the end,
        When humbly we bend
      Our knee, and look upward in ſearch of a friend,
We'll find one aloft ever conſtant and faſt
To the man who through life nails his flag to the maſt.

SPRING TIME.

SPRING time is coming, all laden with flowers,
Spreading her mantle of green o'er the bowers.
The lark, high in air, is beginning to fing
Her fong of rejoicing, to welcome the Spring.
Brooks are flowing,
Life beftowing,
Lovely Nature feems to fling
All her charms,
With willing arms,
In the lap of blooming Spring.

Silver-haired Winter before her is flying,
In the depths of the valley unwept he is dying,—
Save the tears of compaffion that pity may wring
From the bright eyes of April—the infant of Spring.

4

Birds are mating,
Blifs relating,
In each tuneful ftrain they fing;
Hafte, then, deareft!
Love feems neareft,
Holieft, brighteft, in the Spring.

THE YACHTMAN'S SONG.

WAKE, boys, awake ! 'Tis the dawning of day,
The fignal is flying, and we muft away ;
The breeze is faft lifting the mifts from the fea,
And, like fmoke-wreaths, they're drifting away
on our lee.
Quick, loofe all your fails, let the halyards be manned,
And hoift away brifkly, boys, hand over hand ;
Now jump to the windlafs, belay, boys, belay !
Heave hard, now fhe breaks, and the anchor's away.
Then pafs round the bottle, a bumper we'll drain ;
Fill high every goblet with foaming champagne ;
And aye, as we drink, boys, our toaft it fhall be—
The girls that we love, and a life on the fea.

A hand by the helm, up the jib, aft the fheet ;
The wind is ahead, down the bay we muft beat,
But we'll fkim o'er the wave, in the eye of the gale,
While the fpray dafhes high in the luff of our fail.

Keep her clofe to the wind, we are nearing the fhore,
And, hark, on the ftrand how the loud breakers roar.
Quick ready about, put your helm hard a-lee ;
Let fly your jib-fheet, round fhe comes merrily.
  Then pafs round the bottle, &c., &c.

See, fee, boys, the wind is beginning to veer ;
Eafe off every fheet, on our courfe we can fteer ;
Get your fquare-fail acrofs, on your main boom a guy,
Hurrah, boys, hurrah, like a fea-bird we fly.
The wind blows more frefh, and the ftorm-fcud flies low,
Quick, reef every fail, the maft bends like a bow.
Our gallant craft heeds not, though tempefts may rave,
And the lightning with plumes tip the caps of the wave.
  Then pafs round the bottle, &c., &c.

At laft, boys, the long wifhed for haven we near ;
Our friends on the fhore greet our gun with a cheer ;
The anchor let go, flow fwing round to the tide,
Furl the fails, coil the ropes, and fecurely we ride.
Three cheers for our yacht, boys, three cheers for our
  crew,
Three cheers for our flag, boys, the red, white, and blue ;
Three cheers for our club, boys, and as for the reft,
Hurrah, boys, hurrah for the girls we love beft.
  Then pafs round the bottle, &c., &c.

SAM.

O H, my name it is Sam, and my Uncle, d'ye fee,
Is known very well to the world far and near,—
For he's broad and he's long,
And he's tough and he's ftrong,
And he never does wrong,
And he never knows fear.

He grows very faft, does my Uncle, d'ye fee,
Though but a child yet, ne'er a giant's as tall,
And he's bound to expand
O'er the fea and the land,
And he'll ne'er ftop his hand,
Till he's gathered it all.

He never fays die, does my Uncle, d'ye fee,
Ne'er knows when he's whipped, for he never was
taught it,

And when he is right,
He'll continue to fight
Through the day, through the night,
Till the foeman has caught it.

He's a regular brick, is my Uncle, d'ye fee,
And he's bid all the world to his boundlefs poffeffions,
Both the fmall and the great,
So I fear it's too late
To fhut down the gate,
And fhut out their aggreffions.

TEDDY O'MURPHY.

AM Teddy O'Murphy by name,
  My affections will yet be the death of me,—
From the County of Kerry I came,
  For 'twas there that I firſt drew the breath
    of me.
I've a fondneſs for ſweet mountain dew,
  ‧A weakneſs for backy, I'm thinking,
For plenty of nothing to do,
  Save conſtantly eating and drinking.

My affections I place on the ſex,
  Whenever I have opportunity ;
And I'd like very well to annex
  That part of the Mormon community.

Who my firſt ſweetheart was, I forget,—
   'Twas Kate Dennis or Peggy O'Brien,—
The one is a ſpinſter as yet,
   The other ran off with Pat Ryan.

I next courted Molly McGee,
   And I ſwear that I loved her diſtraƈtedly ;
But I quickly got tired, you ſee,
   The courting went on ſo protraƈtedly.
My next flame was Bridget O'Toole,
   And ſhe was the hoighth of benignity,
But ſhe handled a three-legged ſtool
   In a way that offended my dignity.

Now Bridget is Miſtreſs O'Flynn,
   Kate Dennis is Widow O'Mopperty,
With three ſtrapping girls and one twin,
   While Peggy's another man's property.
But there's fiſh as good left in the ſea,
   If a man only knows how to capture them ;
And the girls are all waiting for me,—
   Och, Teddy's the boy to enrapture them.

Chorus of Spirits.

EVENING is falling o'er meadow and lea,
 Flinging its fhadow o'er rock and o'er tree;
 Clouds too are rifing to darken the fcene,
 Veiling the heavens where ftars fhould be feen;
At fuch a time, 'tis ours to come
From the portals of the tomb,
From our far off fpirit home.
  Whether it be
  Beneath the fea,
  Or whether we lay
  In grave yard clay,
  Then gather! gather! gather!
   Spirits of the dead;
  Gather! gather! gather!
   From your grafs-grown bed;
   4*

Gather from the well-filled graves
   Dotting hill and plain;
Gather from the ocean caves
   Where ye long have lain
'Neath the waves.

The ftorm King now marfhals his legions on high,
On the wings of the lightning he rides through the fky;
Lift to the thunder, that bellows afar,
'Tis the found of the wheels of his terrible car;
Summoned every twentieth year,
When the leaf falls yellow and fere,
Brother fpirits we muft gather here.
   Come from the hills!
   Come from the rills!
   Come from the graves!
   Come from the waves!
   Then gather, gather, gather
      'Neath the lightnings bright;
   Gather, gather, gather
      With us here to-night;
   Gather on the mountain fide,
      Let us merry be,
   Make them echo far and wide
      With our jollity
   At even tide.

Song.

.

The day is done,
The fetting fun
Has faded in the weft;
The ftars of night
Are fhining bright,
The birds are gone to reft.
Then brothers dear,
Come gather here,
Each anxious thought refign;
We'll drink the fair,
And drown all care
In the fparkling tears of the vine.

We'll banifh gloom
Till morning come;
Though clouds of forrow lower,
Your goblet fill.
And every ill
Shall own its magic power.
This night fhall glee
Triumphant be,

And rofy wreaths entwine,
　　To crown the bowl,
　　And glad the foul
In the fparkling tears of the vine.

　　Till death draws near,
　　We'll gather here,
And quaff the cup of gladnefs ;
　　Though fortune frown,
　　In wine we'll drown,
Ere breathed, the figh of fadnefs.
　　And when at length,
　　With fading ftrength,
Our life we muft refign,
　　To mem'ries paft,
　　We'll drink our laft,
In the fparkling tears of the vine.

Ballad.

When circled round in youth's glad fpring
　　With friends we love and hearts we prize,
. When buds of hope are bloffoming,
　　And all feems bright as fummer fkies,

Sweet birds fing out from bufh and fpray
   While gayly pafs the fleeting hours,
As down the path of life we ftray,
   We leave the thorns, but pluck the flowers.

But all too foon the fpring is gone,
   And hope with youth and fpring departs;
The winter winds life's path have ftrown
   With withered leaves and withered hearts.
And though in mem'ry oft we tread
   Along the joyous paft again,
We weep for friends and flowers all dead,
   Sorrow and thorns alone remain.

Prayer.

Protecting power, on thee I call;
   To thee for aid I humbly pray;
Surrounding fears my heart appall,
   Which thou alone canft drive away.
My finking fpirit has no guide,
   Save thee alone, and only thee;
I am bereft of all befide;
   Protecting power, oh pity me.

Low before thy footstool bending,
Hear the humble prayer ascending!
God of battles thou defending,
    Vict'ry shall our conflict crown.
By the tears of widows weeping!
By the blood of freemen sleeping!
Take our country to thy keeping!
    On thy suppliants, Lord, look down.

Chorus.

God of battles, hear our prayer!
    Low before thy throne we bow;
Shield us 'neath thy guardian care,
    Lift our supplications now!

God of battles, aid our land!
    Save us in this trying hour,
Support the self-devoted band
    From oppression's mighty power.

God of battles, hear our vow!
    Be it registered on high;
We will free our country now,
    Or unconquered bravely die!

Song.

Come, gather round, my comrades brave,
   And fill each goblet high;
One moment let us turn away
   From thoughts of battle nigh.
And as we each our goblet drain,
   Let memory remind us,
And give a tear to thofe fo dear,
   The friends we've left behind us.

Then be the toaft " To abfent friends!"
   And let the cup run o'er,
For we, perchance, may never hear
   Their loving voices more.
To-morrow dying on the field,
   The fetting fun may find us;
But we fhall fall, beloved by all
   The friends we've left behind us.

Camp Song.

Hurrah for the life the foldier leads,
　　When he fights in his country's caufe;
His fword, the only friend he needs,
　　At Freedom's call he draws.

When the weary march of the day is done,
　　We halt and encamp for the night
By fome river's fide, where the fetting fun
　　Gilds the ftream with its dying light.

We pitch our tents 'neath the fpreading trees,
　　And light our cheerful fires;
To whofe flame the circling infect flees,
　　And, kiffing its death, expires.

We ftation the watch, left the foe fhould come
　　While the worn-out camp repofes;
Then we gather in groups and talk of home,
　　Till the tired eyelid clofes.

With the fun we rife, then away we fpeed,
　　And ere long are in the battle;
On the foe we prefs, and little heed
　　Death-fhots that round us rattle.

At beat of drum, when the fight is done,
We count our leffened number—
And we join in the fhout for battle won,
A tear for the brave who flumber.

Chorus.

Spread our banners to the wind,
For our glorious tafk is done;
Chains no more Columbia bind,
Freedom's fons have fought and won.
Our ftarry flag waves proudly o'er us,
Days of peace rife bright before us,
Echo anfwers back the chorus,
Union, Freedom, Wafhington.

Weep not for the brave who died—
In their country's caufe they fell:
Let the tears of grief be dried—
In their country's heart they dwell.
They have gained immortal glory,
Theirs is an undying ftory;
Smiling youth and grandfire hoary,
Of their glorious deeds fhall tell.

Ballad.

Alone, all alone, in this wide world of forrow,
  No kind friend to comfort, no children to cheer,
No joy for to-day and no hope for to-morrow,
  And gone is each heart that I ever held dear.

All the friends of my youth one by one have departed—
  The tomb-ftones repeat the fad tale that they died ;
My wife, too, is gone, and ere long, broken-hearted,
  I fhall tranquil repofe in the grave by her fide.

Ah, say, are there none that will greet me with gladnefs ?
  Are there none to remind me of happy days paft ?
No, all, all are gone that would grieve at my fadnefs—
  Then welcome the tomb that receives me at laft.

www.ingramcontent.com/pod-product-compliance
Lightning Source LLC
Chambersburg PA
CBHW020305090426
42735CB00009B/1228